by the same author

*

ALBERT'S BRIDGE

A play

by
TOM STOPPARD

FABER AND FABER
3 Queen Square,
London

First published in 1969
as 'Albert's Bridge' and 'If You're Glad I'll be Frank'
by Faber and Faber Limited
3 Queen Square London WC1
First published in this new edition 1970
Reprinted 1977
Printed in Great Britain by
Whitstable Litho Limited, Whitstable, Kent
All rights reserved
ISBN 571 09471 6

© 1969 by Tom Stoppard

Albert's Bridge received its first production on the BBC Third Programme on the 13th July 1967. The cast was as follows:

BOB	Nigel Anthony
CHARLIE	Alexander John
DAD	Geoffery Wincott
ALBERT	John Hurt
CHAIRMAN	Victor Lucas
DAVE	Ian Thompson
GEORGE	Anthony Jackson
FITCH	Ronald Herdman
MOTHER	Betty Hardy
FATHER	Alan Dudley
KATE	Barbara Mitchell
FRASER	Haydn Jones

Produced by Charler Lefeaux

The stage version of *Albert's Bridge* was presented by The Oxford Theatre Group as part of the Edinburgh Festival Fringe 1969. The cast was as follows:

BOB	Michael Forbes
CHARLIE	Michael Baker
DAD	Michael Bevan
ALBERT	Jonathan Levy
CHAIRMAN	Ian Small
DAVID	Alan Franks
GEORGE	David Snodin
FATHER	Jeremy Rycroft
FITCH	Jules Boardman
KATE	Louise Godfrey
FRASER	Graham Billing
ALBERT'S MOTHER	Caroline Lee

Directed by HENRY MURRAY
Designed by GWENDOLYN EUSTACE
Lighting Designer ROBIN GIFFARD
Assistant Director JULES BOARDMAN

The music for *Albert's Bridge* was specially composed for this production by David Stoll.

ALBERT'S BRIDGE

Fade up bridge, with painting on mike. Four men are painting a big girdered railway bridge. They are spaced vertically, in ascending order: BOB, CHARLIE, DAD, ALBERT. *To begin with, the mike is at* ALBERT'*s level, the top.*

BOB (*the most distant*): Char-lee!
CHARLIE (*less distant*): Hel-lo!
BOB: Right Charlie?
CHARLIE: Right! Comin' down! . . . Hey, Dad!
DAD (*an older man, not very distant*): Hel-lo!
CHARLIE: Bob 'n' me is done down here!
DAD: Right!
CHARLIE: Have you done?
DAD: Comin' down! . . . Albert! Al-bert!
CHARLIE (*more distant*): Albert!
BOB (*most distant*): Al-bert!
ALBERT (*very close, crooning softly, tunelessly amid various tunes while painting*):
    How high the moon in June?
    how blue the moon when it's high noon
    and the turtle doves above
    croon out of tune in love
    saying please above the trees
    which when there's thunder you don't run under
    —those trees—
    'cos there'll be pennies fall on Alabama
    and you'll drown in foggy London town
    the sun was shi-ning . . . on my Yiddisher Mama.
BOB (*most distant*): Albert!
CHARLIE (*less distant*): Albert!
DAD (*off*): Albert!
ALBERT: Hel-lo!

7

DAD: Bob 'n' me 'n' Charlie's done!

ALBERT: Right!

Dip-brush-slap-slide-slick, and once again, dip, brush, slap—oh, it goes on so nicely . . . tickle it into the corner, there, behind the rivet. . . . No one will see that from the ground; I could cheat up here. But I'd know; so dip, brush, slap, slide and once again for the last time till the next time—every surface sleek, renewed—dip, brush, slap, slick, tickle and wipe—right in there with the old rust-proof rust-brown—all glossed and even, end to end— the last touch—perfection! (*Painting stops.*) Oh my! I could stand back to admire it and fall three hundred feet into the sea. Mind your heads! (*Laughs. Climbing down.*) Mind your head, Dad!

DAD: I'm not your dad. Keep off the wet—work down the slope to the middle—and watch your feet.

(*Everyone climbing down, the distance between them closing.*) Going down for good, oh yes, I'm not facing that again. Ten coats I've done, end to end, and now I'm done all right. I had ambitions, you know. . . .

CHARLIE (*nearer*): Mind my head, Dad.

DAD: Watch my feet, Charlie—comin' down——

CHARLIE: I'll watch your feet—you mind my head. Watch your head, Bob——

BOB (*nearer*): Watch your feet, Charlie——

CHARLIE: Mind my feet Bob—watch my head, Dad. . . .

DAD: I'm not your dad, and mind my feet—that's my head, Albert.

ALBERT: Comin' down. . . . Doesn't she look beautiful?

DAD: Looks the same as always. There's no progress. Twenty years, twenty thousand pots of paint . . . yes, I had plans.

CHARLIE: I thought we'd never see the end of it.

BOB: It's not the bleeding end.

CHARLIE: There's no end to it.

DAD: Ten coats non-stop, one after the other, and it's no improvement, no change even, just holding its own against the weather—that's a long time, that's a lot of paint. I could have made my mark.

8

ALBERT: Continuity—that's hard to come by.

DAD: I've spread my life over those girders, and in five minutes I could scrape down to the iron, I could scratch down to my prime.

ALBERT: Simplicity—so . . . contained; neat; your bargain with the world, your wages, your time, your energy, your property, everything you took out and everything you put in, the bargain that has carried you this far—all contained there in ten layers of paint, accounted for. Now that's something; to keep track of everything you put into the kitty, to have it lie there, under your eye, fixed and immediate—there are no consequences to a coat of paint. That's more than you can say for a factory man; his bits and pieces scatter, grow wheels, disintegrate, change colour, join up in new forms which he doesn't know anything about. In short, he doesn't know what he's done, to whom.

DAD: Watch your feet, Albert. Mind your head, Charlie.

CHARLIE: You mind my head. Take care my feet, Bob——

BOB: Watch your feet, Charlie——

CHARLIE: Mind your feet, Dad——

DAD: That's my head, Albert——

ALBERT: Coming down. . . .

Ah, look at it up there, criss-crossed and infinite, you can't see where it ends—I could take off and swing through its branches screaming like a gibbon!

DAD: Mind where you're putting your feet, Albert.

CHARLIE: Watch my head, Dad.

BOB: Train coming, Charlie.

(*Distant train coming.*)

CHARLIE: I've seen it.

BOB (*jumping down on to gravel*): And down.

CHARLIE: Mind where you jump, Dad.

DAD: Seen it.

CHARLIE (*jumping down*): None too soon.

DAD: Train coming, Albert.

ALBERT: I'm with you.

DAD (*jumps down*): Finished.

CHARLIE: Like hell.

BOB: Well, that's another two years behind you.

DAD: A feller once offered me a half share in a very nice trading station in the China Seas. I had it in me.

ALBERT: Mind your toes.

(*He jumps. Climbing down ends. All are now on mike.*)

Now that's a good way to end a day—ending so much else.

CHARLIE: All right for some. Students.

BOB: Slummers.

CHARLIE: Pocket-money holiday lads, oh yes.

ALBERT: One bridge—freshly painted—a million tons of iron thrown across the bay—rust brown and even to the last lick—spick and span, rust-proofed, weather-resistant—perfect!

DAD: Other end needs painting now. A man could go mad.

(*The train arrives and goes screaming past.*)

(*Set* CHAIRMAN *over end of train, cutting bridge.*)

CHAIRMAN: Let us not forget, gentlemen, that Clufton Bay Bridge is the fourth biggest single-span double-track shore-to-shore railway bridge in the world bar none——

DAVE: Hear, hear, Mr. Chairman——

CHAIRMAN: Thank you, Dave—

GEORGE: I've been studying these figures, Mr. Chairman——

CHAIRMAN: Just a moment, George. We've got an amenity here in Clufton, that bridge stands for the whole town, quite apart from the money earned in railway dues——

DAVE: Hear, hear, Mr. Chairman——

CHAIRMAN: Thank you, Dave.

GEORGE: According to the City Engineer's figures, Mr. Chairman——

CHAIRMAN: Just a moment, George. When my grandfather built this bridge he didn't spare the brass—and I for one, as chairman of the Clufton Bay Bridge Sub-Committee—entrusted as we are with the upkeep and responsibility of what is a symbol of Clufton's prosperity—I for one do not begrudge the spending of a few extra quid on a lick of paint.

DAVE: Hear, hear, Mr. Chairman.

CHAIRMAN: Thank you, Dave.

GEORGE: I know it's a symbol of your prosperity, Mr. Chairman, but——

CHAIRMAN: That's a highly improper remark, George. Clufton's prosperity is what I said.

DAVE: Hear, hear, Mr. Chairman.

CHAIRMAN: Thank you, Dave.

GEORGE: My mistake, Mr. Chairman—but if Mr. Fitch's figures are correct——

FITCH (*distinctive voice; clipped, confident; rimless spectacles*): My figures are always correct, Mr. Chairman.

CHAIRMAN: Hear that, George? The City Engineer's figures are a model of correctitude.

DAVE: Hear, hear, Mr. Chairman.

CHAIRMAN: Thank you, Dave.

GEORGE: Then this new paint he's recommending is going to cost us four times as much as the paint we've been using up to now.
(*Pause.*)

CHAIRMAN: Four times as much? Money?

DAVE: Hear, hear, Mr. Chairman.

CHAIRMAN: Just a moment, Dave. I don't think your figures are correct, George. Mr. Fitch knows his business.

GEORGE: What business is he in—paint?

CHAIRMAN: That's a highly improper remark, George—er, you're not in the paint business, are you, Mr. Fitch?

FITCH: No, Mr. Chairman.

CHAIRMAN: No, no, of course you're not. You should be ashamed, George.

DAVE: Hear, hear, Mr. Chairman.

CHAIRMAN: Shut up, Dave. Now what about it, Mr. Fitch—is this right what George says?

FITCH: Well, up to a point, Mr. Chairman, yes. But in the long run, no.

CHAIRMAN: Don't fiddle-faddle with me, Fitch. Does this new-fangled paint of yours cost four times as much as the paint we've got, and if so, what's in it for you?

GEORGE: Hear, hear, Mr. Chairman.

11

CHAIRMAN: Thank you, George.

FITCH: To put the matter at its simplest, Mr. Chairman, the new paint costs four times as much and lasts four times as long.

CHAIRMAN: Well, there's your answer, George. It costs four times as much but it lasts four times as long. Very neat, Fitch—I thought we'd got you there.

GEORGE: What's the point, then?

FITCH: Apart from its silvery colour, Mr. Chairman, which would be a pleasanter effect than the present rusty brown, the new paint would also afford a considerable saving, as you can no doubt see.

CHAIRMAN: Everybody see that? Well, I don't.

GEORGE: Nor do I.

DAVE: Hear, hear, George.

GEORGE: Shut up, Dave.

FITCH: If I might explain, gentlemen. As you know, in common with other great bridges of its kind, the painting of Clufton Bay Bridge is a continuous operation. That is to say, by the time the painters have reached the far end, the end they started at needs painting again.

DAVE: I never knew that!

CHAIRMAN AND GEORGE: Shut up, Dave.

FITCH: This cycle is not a fortuitous one. It is contrived by relating the area of the surfaces to be painted—call it A— to the rate of the painting—B—and the durability of the paint—C. The resultant equation determines the variable factor X—i.e. the number of painters required to paint surfaces A at speed B within time C. For example——

CHAIRMAN: E.g.

FITCH: Quite. Er, e.g. with X plus one painters the work would proceed at a higher rate—i.e. B, plus, e.g. Q. However, the factors A and C, the surface area and the lasting quality of the paint remain, of course, constant. The result would be that the painters would be ready to begin painting the bridge for the second time strictly speaking before it needed re-painting. This creates the co-efficient—Waste.

CHAIRMAN: W.

12

FITCH: If you like. This co-efficient belies efficiency, you see.

CHAIRMAN: U.C. You see, George?

GEORGE: OK, I see.

FITCH: To continue. Furthermore, the value of the co-efficient—Waste—is progressive. Let me put it like this, gentlemen. Because the rate of painting is constant, i.e. too fast to allow the paintwork to deteriorate, each bit the men come to requires re-painting even less than the bit before it. You see, they are all the time catching up on themselves progressively, until there'll come a point where they'll be re-painting the bridge, while it's still wet! (*Pause.*) No that can't be right. . . .

CHAIRMAN: Come to the point Fitch. Wake up, Dave.

DAVE (*waking up*): Hear, hear, Mr. Chairman.

FITCH: To put it another way, gentlemen, that is to say, conversely. With one too few painters—X minus one—the rate of progress goes down to let us say, B minus Q. So what is the result? By the time the painters are ready to start re-painting, the end they started at has deteriorated into unsightly and damaging rust—a co-efficient representing the converse inefficiency.

CHAIRMAN: Pull yourself together, Fitch—I don't know what you're drivellin' about.

GEORGE: In a nutshell, Fitch—the new paint costs four times as much and lasts four times as long. Where's the money saved?

FITCH: We sack three painters.

(*Pause.*)

CHAIRMAN: Ah. . . .

FITCH: You see, to date we have achieved your optimum efficiency by employing four men. It takes them two years to paint the bridge, which is the length of time the paint lasts. This new paint will last eight years, so we only need one painter to paint the bridge by himself. After eight years, the end he started at will be just ready for re-painting. The saving to the ratepayers would be £3,529 15s. 9d. per annum.

GEORGE: Excuse me, Mr. Chairman——

CHAIRMAN: Just a moment, George. I congratulate you, Mr. Fitch. An inspired stroke. We'll put it up to the meeting of the full council.

GEORGE: Excuse me——

CHAIRMAN: Shut up, George.

DAVE: Hear, hear, Mr. Chairman.

FITCH: Thank you, Mr. Chairman.

CHAIRMAN: Thank you, Mr. Fitch.

(*Fade.*)

MOTHER: Aren't you getting up, Albert? It's gone eleven. . . . Are you listening to me, Albert?

ALBERT (*in bed*): What?

MOTHER: I'm talking to you, Albert.

ALBERT: Yes?

MOTHER: Yes-what?

ALBERT: Yes, Mother.

MOTHER: That's better. Oh dear, what was I saying?

ALBERT: I don't know, Mother.

MOTHER (*sighs*): I was against that university from the start.

ALBERT: The country needs universities.

MOTHER: I mean it's changed you, Albert. You're thinking all the time. It's not like you, Albert.

ALBERT: Thinking?

MOTHER: You don't talk to me. Or your father. Well, I'm glad it's all behind you, I hope it starts to wear off.

ALBERT: I wanted to stay on after my degree, but they wouldn't have me.

MOTHER: I don't know what you want to know about philosophy for. Your father didn't have to study philosophy, and look where he is, Chairman of Metal Alloys and Allied Metals. It's not as if you were going to be a philosopher or something. . . . Yes, you could have been a trainee executive by now. As it is you'll have to do your stint on the factory floor, philosophy or no philosophy. That university has held you back.

ALBERT: I'll have to get myself articled to a philosopher. . . .

14

Start at the bottom. Of course, a philosopher's clerk
wouldn't get the really interesting work straight off, I know
that. It'll be a matter of filing the generalizations, tidying
up the paradoxes, laying out the premises before the boss
gets in—that kind of thing; but after I've learned the ropes
I might get a half share in a dialectic, perhaps, and work
up towards a treatise. . . . Yes, I could have my own
thriving little philosopher's office in a few years.
(*Pause.*)

MOTHER: Would you like to have some coffee downstairs?

ALBERT: Yes.

MOTHER: Yes-what?

ALBERT: Yes please.

(*Pause.*)

MOTHER: I still think it was mean of you not to let us know you
had a summer vacation.

ALBERT: I thought you knew. I've had one every year.

MOTHER: You know I've no head for dates. You could have
come home to see us.

ALBERT: I'm sorry—there was this temporary job going. . . .

MOTHER: Your father would have given you some money if
you'd asked him.

ALBERT: I thought I'd have a go myself.

MOTHER: You'll have to get up now.

ALBERT: It was fantastic up there. The scale of it. From the
ground it looks just like a cat's cradle, from a distance you
can take it all in, and then up there in the middle of it the
thinnest threads are as thick as your body and you could
play tennis on the main girders.

MOTHER: Kate will be up in a minute to make the beds.

ALBERT: It's absurd, really, being up there, looking down on the
university lying under you like a couple of bricks, full of
dots studying philosophy——

MOTHER: I don't want you getting in Kate's way—she's got to
clean.

ALBERT: What could they possibly know? I saw more up there
in three weeks than those dots did in three years. I saw the
context. It reduced philosophy and everything else. I got a

perspective. Because that bridge was—separate—complete—removed, defined by principles of engineering which makes it stop at a certain point, which compels a certain shape, certain joints—the whole thing utterly fixed by the rules that make it stay up. It's complete, and a man can give his life to its maintenance, a very fine bargain.

MOTHER: Do you love me, Albert?

ALBERT: Yes.

MOTHER: Yes-what?

ALBERT: Yes please.

(*Cut to a gavel banged on table.*)

MAYORAL VOICE: Number 43 on the order paper, proposal from Bridge sub-committee. . . .

VOICE 1: Move. . . .

VOICE 2: Second.

MAYORAL VOICE: All in favour.

(*Absent-minded murmur of fifty 'Ayes'.*)

Against. (*Pause.*) Carried. Number 44 on the order paper. (*Fade.*)

(*Fade up knock on door off. Door opens.*)

KATE: Oh, I'm sorry, Mr. Albert.

ALBERT: Hello, I was just thinking of getting up.

(*Cut to.*)

BOB: What—by myself? It would take years.

FITCH: Eight years, yes.

BOB: No. I demand a transfer.

FITCH: I thought I'd give you first refusal.

BOB: I want to go back to painting the Corporation crest on the dustcarts.

FITCH: I could fit you in on the magenta.

BOB: On the what?

FITCH: It's one man to a colour nowadays. Efficiency.

(*Cut.*)

CHARLIE: You must be joking.

16

FITCH: It's an opportunity for you.

CHARLIE: I'd go mad. What's it all about?

FITCH: Efficiency.

CHARLIE: I'm not doing that bridge on me tod.

FITCH: It's no more work than before.

CHARLIE: I'd jump off within a month.

FITCH: Oh. Well, we couldn't have that. That would be only one ninety-sixth of it done.

(*Cut.*)

DAD: You mean it's a cheaper way of doing it.

FITCH: More efficient.

DAD: We've been doing a good job.

FITCH: Efficiency isn't a matter of good and bad, entirely. It's a matter of the optimum use of resources—time, money, manpower.

DAD: You mean it's cheaper. I'm an old man.

FITCH: You've got eight years in you.

DAD: It might be my last eight. I haven't done anything yet— I've got a future.

FITCH: Well, I could put you on yellow no-parking lines.

DAD: Yes, all right.

(*Cut.*)

FITCH: . . . But do you have any qualifications?

ALBERT: I've got a degree in philosophy, Mr. Fitch.

FITCH: That's a little unusual.

ALBERT: I wouldn't say that. There were lots of us doing it.

FITCH: That's all very well if you're going to be a philosopher, but what we're talking about is painting bridges.

ALBERT: Yes, yes, I can see what you're driving at, of course, but I don't suppose it did me any harm. Almost everyone who didn't know what to do, did philosophy. Well, that's logical.

FITCH: You're an educated man.

ALBERT: Thank you.

FITCH: What I mean is, you're not the run-of-the-mill bridge painter, not the raw material I'm looking for.

17

ALBERT: Well, I did it in the vacation.

FITCH: Yes . . . yes, I did have reports of you. But surely. . . .

ALBERT: I know what you mean, but that's what I want to do. I liked it. I don't want to work in a factory or an office.

FITCH: Is it the open air life that attracts you?

ALBERT: No. It's the work, the whole thing—crawling round that great basket, so high up, being responsible for so much that is so visible. Actually I don't know if that's why I like it. I like it because I was happy up there, doing something simple but so grand, without end. It doesn't get away from you.

FITCH: The intellectual rather than the practical—that's it, is it?

ALBERT: Probably.

FITCH: I'm the same. It's poetry to me—a perfect equation of space, time and energy——

ALBERT: Yes——

FITCH: It's not just slapping paint on a girder——

ALBERT: No——

FITCH: It's continuity—control—mathematics.

ALBERT: Poetry.

FITCH: Yes, I should have known it was a job for a university man. . . .

ALBERT: Like me and you——

FITCH: Well, I went to night school myself.

ALBERT: Same thing, different time.

FITCH: That's what I say.

ALBERT: I'm your man, Mr. Fitch.

FITCH: You'll stick to it for eight years, will you?

ALBERT: Oh, I'll paint it more than once.

(*Cut.*)

(*Breakfast in background.*)

FATHER: Now then, Albert, you've had your fun. When I was your age I'd got six years of work behind me.

ALBERT: Well, I'm starting work now, father.

FATHER: Quite so, but don't think you're going to start at the top. You'll get there all right in time but you've got to learn the business first. Is there any more tea, Mother?

18

MOTHER: Ring for Kate, would you, Albert?

ALBERT (*going*): Yes, mother.

MOTHER: That reminds me.

FATHER: You'll start where I started. On the shop floor.

ALBERT (*approach*): Well, actually, Father——

MOTHER: I don't want to sound Victorian, but one can't just turn a blind eye.

ALBERT: What?

FATHER: Yes, I never went in for books and philosophy and look at me now.

MOTHER: I suppose that's the penance one pays for having servants nowadays.

ALBERT: What?

FATHER: I started Metal Alloys and Allied Metals—built it up from a biscuit-tin furnace in the back garden, small smelting jobs for the cycle-repair shop.

MOTHER: I've suspected her for some time and now one can't ignore it. Even with her corset.

ALBERT: Who?

FATHER: You can come in on Monday and I'll hand you over to the plant foreman.

ALBERT: I've already got a job. Actually.

FATHER: You haven't got a job till I give you one.

ALBERT: I'm going to paint Clufton Bay Bridge, starting Monday.

MOTHER: What colour?

ALBERT: Silver.

FATHER: Just a minute——

KATE (*off*): You rang, madam?

MOTHER: More tea, Kate, please.

KATE: Yes, madam.

MOTHER: And a word.

KATE: Yes, madam.

MOTHER: Are you ill?

KATE: No, madam.

MOTHER: I believe I heard you being ill in the bathroom, this morning.

KATE: Yes, madam.

19

MOTHER: And yesterday?

KATE: Yes, madam.

ALBERT: What's the matter, Kate?

KATE: Nothing, Mr. Albert.

MOTHER: Leave this to me. Cook tells me you fainted in the kitchen last week.

KATE: I came over funny.

ALBERT: Kate. . . .

MOTHER: Let's not beat about the bush. Is it the gardener's boy?

KATE: No, madam.

MOTHER: Then who is it?

ALBERT: Who's what?

MOTHER: Well, I'm sorry. You can have a month's wages, of course. You'd better make sure that the young man does the right thing by you.
(*Cut.*)

KATE: I never thought you'd do the right thing by me, Albert.

ALBERT: We'll be all right. It's a nice room.

KATE: Your mum didn't like it.

ALBERT: My mother's got no taste. I'll make a fire.

KATE: And wrap up warm when you go out—it'll be freezing up there.

ALBERT: Only a breeze.

KATE: It'll be ice in a month. If you fell I'd die, Albert.

ALBERT: So would I.

KATE: Don't you ever fall. They shouldn't make it a year-round job. It's dangerous.

ALBERT: No—you don't know how big it is—the threads are like ladders and the cross-pieces are like piers into the sky.

KATE: You hold on tight, for the spring, and the baby.
(*Cut in bridge and painting.*)

ALBERT: Slip, slap, brush, dip, slop, slide, slick and wipe. . . . In eight years I'll be pushing thirty, and the Clufton Bay Bridge will be a silver bridge—dip-brush, slick, slide, slap without end, I'm the bridge man,

20

web-spinning silvering spiderman
crawling between heaven and earth on a
cantilevered span,
cat's cradled in the sky . . .
look down at the toy ships
where the sea pounds under toy trains to
toy towns
under my hand.
Am I the spider or the fly?
I'm the bridge man. . . .

The downstairs maid went upstairs to make a bed that I
was in—and suddenly——
(*Cut out bridge. Cut in crying baby.*)

I name this child Albert.

KATE: You can't.

ALBERT: Very well. I name this child Kate.

KATE: Katherine.

ALBERT: Tomorrow wheel her along to the bridge so I can see
you.

KATE: All right. But don't wave, Albert. Don't wave. If you
waved and fell——

ALBERT: I shan't wave.

(*Cut in bridge and painting.*)
Dip brush, dip brush
without end, come rain or shine;
A fine way to spend my time.
My life is set out for me,
the future traced in brown,
my past measured in silver;
how absurd, how sublime
(don't look down)
to climb and clamber in a giant frame;
dip brush, dip brush, slick, slide wipe
and again.
(*Painting stops.*)
I straddle a sort of overflowing gutter on which bathtub

boats push up and down. . . . The banks are littered with various bricks, kiddiblocks with windows; dinky toys move through the gaps, dodged by moving dots that have no colour; under my feet the Triang train thunders across the Meccano, and the minibrick estates straggle up over the hill in neat rows with paintbox gardens. It's the most expensive toytown in the store—the detail is remarkable. But fragile. I tremble for it, half expecting some petulant pampered child to step over the hill and kick the whole thing to bits with her Startrite sandals.

(*Painting.*)

Don't look down,
the dots are looking up.
Don't wave, don't fall, tumbling down a
telescope, diminishing to a dot.
In eight years who will I be?
Not me.
I'll be assimilated then,
the honest working man, father of three—
you've seen him around,
content in his obscurity, come to terms with public truths,
digging the garden of a council house
in what is now my Sunday suit.
I'm okay for fifty years, with any luck;
I can see me climb
up a silver bridge to paint it for the seventh time,
keeping track of my life spent in painting in the colour of
   my track:
above it all.
How sublime
(dip brush, dip brush) silvering the brown.
Which dot is mine?
Don't wave, don't look down.
Don't fall.

(*Cut bridge.*)

KATE: I saw you today.
ALBERT: What was I doing?

KATE: Painting, I suppose. Crawling backwards along a cross-piece.

ALBERT: Pulling silver after me. I didn't see you. Or I didn't see which one was you.

KATE: Coming out of the hairdressers. Six and six, I had it cut.

ALBERT: Just goes to show—if you get far enough away, six and sixpence doesn't show, and nor does anything, at a distance.

KATE: Well, life is all close up, isn't it?

ALBERT: Yes, it hits you, when you come back down. How close it all is. You can't stand back to look at it.

KATE: Do you like my hair like this?

ALBERT: Like what? Oh—yes. Do you like mine?

KATE: I got whistled at in the street.

ALBERT: It's always happening to me.

KATE: A lorry driver, at the traffic lights.

ALBERT: They're the worst, I find.

KATE: Oh, Albert. I had the pram with me too.

ALBERT: You look too young for it. Big sister.

KATE: And I cook very nice, don't I?

ALBERT: I'd whistle at you.

KATE: I'd come, if you whistled. I'd give you a wink and say, 'Cheeky!'

ALBERT: Oh, yes—you'd get off with me. No trouble at all. I'd take you down by the canal after the pictures.

KATE: What do you know about it—with your education and all?

ALBERT: Me? I'm a working man.

KATE: You don't have regrets, do you, Albert?

ALBERT: No.

KATE: It wasn't a good bargain, on the face of it.

ALBERT: It depends on what you want.

KATE: Me and the baby. Two rooms and a forty-five hour week, hard work and no advancement.

ALBERT: I'm not ambitious.

KATE: You could have had so much—a white wedding, nice house, an office job with real prospects, the country club ... tennis. ... Yes, you could have had Metal Alloys and Allied Metals—the top job, responsibility, your own office

23

with telephones. . . .

ALBERT: Yes, I'm well out of that.

(*Cut in bridge and painting.*)

Progress. Two lines of silver meeting in an angle bracket—
—and tickle in there behind the rivet—slip slop and wipe
and on we go up the slope.

Does the town look up? Do they all gawp and say to each
other, look at him! How ridiculous he looks up there, so
small, how laughably inadequate. Or do they say, How
brave! One man against the elements! Pitted against so
much!

The lone explorer feeling his way between the iron
crevasses, tacked against the sky by his boots and fingers.
Dots, bricks and beetles.

I could drown them in my spit.

(*Cut bridge, cut in baby's rattle in background.*)

KATE: That isn't nice, Albert.

ALBERT: Spitting?

KATE: Talking like that.

ALBERT: It doesn't represent desire. I'll let them live. I'm only
trying to tell you what it's like.

KATE: I know what it's like. It's painting a girder. There's other
jobs.

ALBERT: It's my bridge—I wish you'd stop her rattling, it's
getting on my nerves.

KATE: That's very advanced for six months.

ALBERT: I'm not doubting her progress. If she played the
trumpet it would be even more advanced but it would still
be sending me round the twist. Here, give——

(*He dispossesses the rattler, who bawls.*)

KATE: Now you've set her off. She doesn't *understand.*
(*Comforting.*) Come on, then. . . .

ALBERT: Well, see you later.

KATE: Where are you going?

ALBERT: Work.

KATE: It's your Saturday off.

ALBERT: No, it's my Saturday on.
KATE: Last Saturday was your Saturday on.
ALBERT: Well, I'll take two off in a row.

> (*Cut in bridge.*)
> Listen . . .
> The hot sun makes you think of insects,
> but this insect hum is the whole city
> caught in a seashell. . . .
> All conversation is hidden there,
> among motors, coughing fits, applause,
> screams, laughter, feet on the stairs,
> secretaries typing to dictation,
> radios delivering the cricket scores,
> tapes running, wheels turning, mills grinding,
> chips frying, lavatories flushing, lovers sighing,
> the mayor blowing his nose.
> All audible life in the vibration
> of a hairdryer in the room below.
> (*Painting.*)
> Dip brush, slide, stroke,
> it goes on as smooth and shiny
> as my sweat. I itch.
> Paint on my arm,
> silver paint on my brown arm;
> it could be part of the bridge.
> (*Painting stops.*)
> Listen. The note of Clufton is B flat.
> The whole world could be the same.
> Look down. Is it a fact
> that all the dots have names?
> (*Cut bridge.*)

KATE: Jack Morris is taking Maureen and little Leslie to Paris.
ALBERT: Who's Jack Morris?
KATE: Next door, Albert.
ALBERT: Oh yes. Who's Maureen?
KATE: Mrs. Morris.

ALBERT: So little Leslie would be their little girl.

KATE: It's a little boy.

ALBERT: Ah. Why are we talking about them?

KATE: They're going to Paris for a holiday. Where are we going?

ALBERT: When?

KATE: That's what I'd like to know.

ALBERT: What?

KATE: Don't you have a holiday?

ALBERT: Oh. I suppose I must. Everybody does. Yes, I expect Fitch took that into account.

KATE: You're not going to dodge your holiday—I know what you're up to, you're already working full Saturdays, don't think I'm such a fool that I don't know. . . . And you're working till dark.

ALBERT: Overtime. I lose time in the winter.

KATE (*sniffing*): It's because you don't like it here, being at home.

ALBERT: Oh, Kate . . . I've got a schedule, you see.

KATE: You're miles ahead of it.

ALBERT: I've got to have some in hand in case of accidents.

KATE: I told you! You'll fall off, and me and Katherine will be alone.

ALBERT: No, no, no . . . stop crying. We'll have a holiday. I'll take a week.

KATE: A fortnight.

ALBERT: All right, I don't mind.

KATE: Can we go to Paris?

ALBERT: I've been to Paris. There's nothing there, believe me. We could go to Scotland.

KATE: Touring?

ALBERT: Certainly. The Firth of Forth.

KATE: We haven't got a car. Maureen said we could go with them.

ALBERT: But they're going to Paris.

KATE: We could afford it. It wouldn't be hard, it's easier with two children and joined forces. . . . It would be lovely, I've always wanted to see the Champs Elysee and the Ark de Triumph and the Seine and the Eiffel Tower. . . .

(*Cliché French accordion music. Cross-fade to Eiffel Tower. It's the same as Clufton Bridge.*)

(*Distant. Shouting up.*) Albert! A-a-albert! (*Repeated, fading, despairing.*) Come down! Please come down!

ALBERT: I thought as much. Dots, bricks, beetles . . . in B flat. Still, I'm glad I came. The pointlessness takes one's breath away—a tower connects nothing, it stands only so that one can go up and look down. Bridge-builders have none of this audacity, compromise themselves with function. Monsieur Eiffel, poet and philosopher, every eight years I'll scratch your name in the silver of Clufton Bay Bridge.

KATE (*distant, despairing*): Al-bert!

ALBERT (*quiet*): Coming down.

(*Cut Eiffel Tower.*)

(*Crockery smashes, flung against wall.*)

KATE: What's her name?

ALBERT: Kate. . . .

KATE: What a bloody coincidence!

ALBERT: You've got it all wrong, Kate, there's no woman——

KATE (*crying*): I can smell her on your coat!

ALBERT: It's paint—I tell you I was up on the bridge.

KATE: All night!

ALBERT: I just thought I would. It was nice up there.

KATE: You're barmy if you expect me to believe that, you're round the twist——

ALBERT: It's true——

KATE: And I believe it, I *am* round the twist! I'm as barmy as you are, but I believe it——

ALBERT: That's better——

(*Another cup smashes.*)

KATE: No it isn't—it's worse! A woman would be normal. (*Breaking down.*) You don't talk to me, you don't talk to Katherine, you can't wait to get out of the house and up your favourite girder. (*Quieter, sobbing.*) You don't like me any more, I know you don't—I'm boring for you, I haven't got what you want, and you don't want to hear the things

I tell you because I've got nothing to tell you, nothing happens. . . .

ALBERT: I like a quiet life, that's all.

KATE: Gutless. You'll spend your whole life painting that bridge. . . .

ALBERT: It's a good job.

KATE: You know damn well it's a stupid job which any thick idiot could do—but you're educated, Albert. You had opportunities. There was Metal Alloys and Allied Metals— you could have gone right up the ladder—we'd have a house, and friends, and we'd entertain and Katherine would have nice friends—you could have been an executive!

ALBERT: I was lying in bed one day when the maid came in to make it. . . . She was all starchy. When she moved, her skirt sort of crackled against her nylons. . . . I never had any regrets, but I did want her to be happy too.

KATE (*sobbing*): I've begun talking to myself, over the sink and stove. . . . I talk to myself because nobody else listens, and you won't talk to me, so I talk to the sink and the stove and the baby, and maybe one day one of them will answer me.

(*Baby gurgles, almost a word.*)

(*Cut to bridge and painting.*)

ALBERT (*crooning flatly amid and around the tune of 'Night and Day*'):

Night and day, I am the one . . .
day and night, I'm really a part of me. . . .
I've got me under my skin.
So why
don't I take all of me
When I begin the beguine. . . .
I get accustomed to my face,
The thought of me makes me stop
before I begin
Yes, I've got me under my skin,
and I get a kick out of me. . . .

28

Day and night, night and day. . . .
Shall I compare me to a summer's day,
'Cos I can't get me out of my mind
I saw me in Monterey . . .
and I'm all right by me,
yes I'm all right, I'm all right,
I'm all right by me. . . .
(*Applause, two-handed, from quite close. Painting stops.*)
Who's there? Who's that?

FRASER (*applauding*): Very nice, very nice. The egotist school of
songwriting.

ALBERT: Who are you?

FRASER: You mean my name?

ALBERT: I suppose so.

FRASER: Fraser.

ALBERT: What are you doing on my bridge?

FRASER: Yours?

ALBERT: I'm painting it. I'm authorized.

FRASER: You've got a big job ahead of you.

ALBERT: I've got the time.

FRASER: You've got the time perhaps, but I'd say that time is
against you. The condition of the paintwork is very
shoddy.

ALBERT: Well, it hasn't been done for a fair while.

FRASER: Yes, it's beginning to look definitely tatty.

ALBERT: I'm getting through it bit by bit.

FRASER: Too slow. The old paint isn't lasting. People have
noticed, you know. There's been talk.

ALBERT: Look here—are you the bridge inspector or something.

FRASER: What?

ALBERT: Did Mr. Fitch send you?

FRASER: Who?

ALBERT: What's it all about then?

FRASER: Look down there. I came up because up was the only
direction left. The rest has been filled up and is still filling.
The city is a hold in which blind prisoners are packed wall
to wall. Motor-cars nose each other down every street, and
they are beginning to breed, spread, they press the people

to the walls by their knees, pinning them by their knees, and there's no end to it, because if you stopped making them, thousands of people would be thrown out of work, and they'd have no money to spend, the shopkeepers would get caught up in it, and the farms and factories, and all the people dependent on them, with their children and all. There's too much of everything, but the space for it is constant. So the shell of human existence is filling out, expanding, and it's going to go bang.

ALBERT: You're frightened of traffic?

FRASER: We are at the mercy of a vast complex of moving parts, any of which might fail. Civilization is in decline, and the white rhino is being wiped out for the racket in bogus aphrodisiacs.

ALBERT: An animal lover——

FRASER: That was merely a trifle I snatched at in my inability to express the whole. I have never been able to understand, for instance, why anyone should want to be a dentist. I cannot pin down the divinity which ensures that just so many people take up dentistry and just so many agree to milk the cows which would otherwise scream in pain just as children would scream if there were no dentists.

ALBERT: I see. A lunatic, in fact.

FRASER: Not certifiably so. By no means certified. I am simply open, wide open, to certain insights. I do not believe that there is anyone in control. There is the semblance of pattern—supply meeting demand, one-way streets, give and take, the presumption of return tickets, promises to pay the bearer on demand, etcetera—but there's nothing really holding it together. One is forced to recognize the arbitrariness of what we claim to be order. Somewhere there is a lynch pin, which, when removed, will collapse the whole monkey-puzzle. And I'm not staying there till it happens.

ALBERT: I see. Well, we all have our problems, but I don't see how that justifies you climbing about council property. So would you kindly descend——

FRASER: That's what I came up for.

ALBERT: To descend?

FRASER: It never occurred to me to stay.

ALBERT: You came up to go down?

FRASER: To jump.

ALBERT: Jump?

FRASER: Off.

ALBERT: Jump off? You'd kill yourself. Ah.

FRASER: Yes.

ALBERT: I see. All right, then.

FRASER: My mind was made up——

ALBERT: I see your point.

FRASER: It seemed the easiest thing to do.

ALBERT: I agree. Well then, time is hurrying by, waiting for no man. Or is that tide?

FRASER: I see you're trying to humour me. Well, I expected that. You'll be sending for a priest next.

ALBERT: Come, come, don't procrastinate.

FRASER: Me?

ALBERT: You said you were going to jump.

FRASER: Well?

ALBERT: Well, jump.

FRASER: Aren't you going to try to talk me out of it?

ALBERT: You know your own mind. And you're holding me up. I've got to paint where you're standing.

FRASER: You wouldn't just stand there without lifting a finger?

ALBERT: I knew it. You're just a talker. Those ones never do it.

FRASER: I can't believe it. You wouldn't just stand there and watch me kill myself.

ALBERT: I thought that's what you wanted.

FRASER: Well, I did. I couldn't bear the noise, and the chaos. I couldn't get free of it, the enormity of that disorder, so dependent on a chance sequence of action and reaction. So I started to climb, to get some height, you know, enough height to drop from, to be sure, and the higher I climbed, the more I saw and the less I heard. And look now. I've been up here for hours, looking down and all it is, is dots and bricks, giving out a gentle hum. Quite safe. Quite

31

small after all. Quite ordered, seen from above. Laid out in squares, each square a function, each dot a functionary. I really think it might work. Yes, from a vantage point like this, the idea of society is just about tenable.

ALBERT: Funked it. Well, mind how you go. Don't fall.
(*Cut bridge.*)

CHAIRMAN: Gentlemen. This special emergency meeting of the Clufton Bay Bridge Sub-Committee has been called as a result of public representations, both direct and via the press, concerning the unsightly condition of what is the symbol of Clufton's prosperity. My grandfather, who was loved by the public, and owed everything to them, must be turning in his grave. It is a salutary reminder that we are all servants of the public, Mr. Fitch.

DAVE: Hear hear, Mr. Chairman.

CHAIRMAN: Shut up, Dave. As chairman, I, of course, take full responsibility. That is the duty of the chairman, regardless of where that responsibility actually lies, Mr. Fitch.

GEORGE: Hear hear, Mr. Chairman.

CHAIRMAN: It is no smiling matter, George. The city publicity officer has been on to me, the Parks and Amenities have been on to me, British Railways have been on to me and the *Clufton Chronicle* has been doing its damndest to get on to me. This committee is the shame and the laughing stock of the Clufton Council, and as the future—as a possible future Mayor, I am gravely embarrassed by having to carry the can for a lack of foresight and watchfulness on the part of committee members whose names I will not mention, George. I have issued a statement to the effect that the squalid state of disrepair of Clufton's highly-respected bridge is the result of a miscalculation by a senior public official, for which I, as chairman, take full responsibility, Mr. Fitch.

FITCH (*a broken man*): I can only say in mitigation that I have been under pressure—a sick man—domestic and financial worries——

CHAIRMAN: Quite, quite. Let's stick to essentials. Two years ago,

32

at your insistence and against my better judgement, which I left unspoken in deference to your professional capacity, we arranged to switch to improved paint lasting eight years, and through a reasoning which I never pretended to follow, to sack three of the four painters. Today, two years later, we are left with a bridge that is only one quarter painted while the other three-quarters is in a condition ranging from the sub-standard to the decrepit. Now then—what happened?

FITCH: Mr. Chairman, gentlemen, I have served Clufton man and boy for five years. . . . Clufton is the repository of my dreams and boyhood memories, the temple of my hopes to transform the running of a living community to a thing of precision and efficiency, a cybernetic poem—a programmed machine as perfect as a rose——

CHAIRMAN: For God's sake, Fitch, pull yourself together.

FITCH: Gentlemen, let us take as our starting point the proposition that X painters painting at the rate of Y would take Z years to paint surface ABC. We found that when X equalled four, Z equalled two, Y and ABC remaining constant. Then along came factor P, a paint lasting eight years——

CHAIRMAN: I can't stand it.

GEORGE: I think what Mr. Fitch is getting at Mr. Chairman is that the brown paint on the bridge was only supposed to last two years, the time that it took four painters to finish the job and start again. Well, of course, when we cut down to one painter using eight-year paint, it was obvious that in two years' time he'd only be a quarter of the way along, so the old paint would be ready for another coat.

CHAIRMAN: If it was obvious why didn't you say so?

GEORGE: I couldn't catch the eye of the chairman. Of course, if we could hang on for another six years, Mr. Fitch would emerge triumphantly vindicated as the poet of precision and efficiency.

CHAIRMAN: I might be dead in six years.

DAVE: Hear hear, Mr. Chairman.

CHAIRMAN: Thank you, Dave. So what are we going to do about it? Fitch?

33

FITCH: Er. . . . If we hired extra painters, one to start at the far end, one in the middle going one way, another going the opposite way, no . . . er, the progressive element intercedes —if we have two painters back to back at a point nine-sixteenths from the far end—no——

CHAIRMAN: We'd better go back to the old system and hire three more painters. Carry on from there.

FITCH: You can't do that! They wouldn't be quick enough on the one hand and they'd finish too soon on the other—you see, the bridge won't need re-painting for another six years, and the resultant coefficient—waste and unsightliness—the entire system would disintegrate and cost thousands——

CHAIRMAN: Money? (*Appalled.*) My grandfather——

GEORGE: I think I see a way out, Mr. Chairman. From the points of view of efficiency and expediency, I think we can get the whole thing resolved with just a bit of organization.

FITCH: Every day counts.

GEORGE: One day is all we'll need.

(*Cut.*)

ALBERT: Met a feller up on the bridge the other day.

KATE (*strained*): Oh yes?

ALBERT: Yes. Climbed up to chuck himself off.

KATE: Did he?

ALBERT: No. Once he got up there, the mood passed.

KATE: Albert. . . .

ALBERT (*going*): Just off.

KATE: You used to say good-bye.

(*Cut to bridge.*)

FRASER: Hello.

ALBERT: Who's that?

FRASER: Me again.

ALBERT: Did you forget something?

FRASER: No, it all came back to me. After I went down, it all started again. So I came back up.

ALBERT: To jump?

FRASER: Yes.

34

ALBERT: Go on then.

FRASER: I'm all right again now. I don't want to.

ALBERT: Now look here, this isn't a public right of way. I'll report you.

FRASER: I can't help it. I'm forced up and coaxed down. I'm a victim of perspective.

ALBERT (*shouts*): Get down!

FRASER: All right, I'm going.

(*Cut bridge.*)

ALBERT: I'm not a complaining man. I let people get on with their own lives, I'm sympathetic to problems, but a line must be drawn. I've found him up there four times now, Mr. Fitch, and each time it's the same story—he doesn't want to jump after all. I've given him every chance.

FITCH: Yes yes, but that isn't what I've asked to see you about at all. You haven't been listening to me.

ALBERT: It's unnerving me, finding company up there. Well, it's changing the character of the job, and playing hell with my schedule—simply on the level of efficiency I protest.

FITCH: Well, as I say, for the reasons given, the matter is to be resolved. We have to get the bridge finished by the end of the week.

ALBERT: What?

FITCH: We can't allow further deterioration. The public is roused.

ALBERT: Wait a minute—I can't possibly finish by the end of the week.

FITCH: I realize, of course, you'll need help. I have made arrangements.

ALBERT: What arrangements?

FITCH: Eighteen-hundred painters will report for work at seven o'clock tomorrow morning. By nightfall the job will be done. I have personally worked it out, and my department has taken care of the logistics.

ALBERT: Eighteen-hundred?

FITCH: Seventeen-hundred-and-ninety-nine. I kept a place for you. I thought you'd like that.

(*Cut to door slam.*)

ALBERT (*breathless*): They're moving in on me, the dots are
    ganging up. I'll need food and spare clothes, a couple of
    blankets. What are you doing?

KATE (*off*): Packing, Albert. I'm going.

ALBERT: Kate, they've got it in for me. They're trying to move
    me off—and I've earned my position. I've worked for it.

KATE (*approach*): I've got a position—a housemaid, living in.
    With Katherine. I'll let you know my days off, for visiting.
    (*Pause.*)

ALBERT: Kate . . . I'm sorry. . . . Will you come and see me
    sometimes. . . . ? Will you come along and wave?

(*Cut in bridge and painting.*)
(*More rapid than before.*)
Dip brush, dip brush—slap it on, slide silver
over the iron, glide like mercury—slick, wipe
tickle it wet, swish, slop, sweep and wipe the
silver slime, it's all I can do—
in eight years I'll be pushing thirty-two
a manic painter coming through for the second time.
Dip brush, dip brush—

FRASER: What's the rush?

(*Painting stops.*)

ALBERT: Fraser.

FRASER: You're going at it.

ALBERT (*shouting*): Get down! Get down!

FRASER: This isn't like you at all.

ALBERT: I'm not having you up here.

FRASER: There's room for both of us.

ALBERT: You're just the first, and I'm not going to have it. If
    you're going to jump—jump.

FRASER: That's why I came, again.

ALBERT (*closer and quieter*): You're going to jump?

FRASER: No. Not today.

ALBERT (*furious*): Up and down like a yo-yo!

FRASER: I agree that it is ludicrous. Down there I am assailed by
    the flying splinters of a world breaking up at the speed of

procreation without end. The centre cannot hold and the outside edge is filling out like a balloon, without the assurance of infinity. More men are hungry than honest, and more eat than produce. The apocalypse cannot be long delayed.

ALBERT: You'd be better out of it. I'll tell them why you did it, if that's what worrying you.

FRASER: . . . So I climb up again and prepare to cast myself off, without faith in angels to catch me—or desire that they should—and lo! I look down at it all and find that the proportions have been re-established. My confidence is restored, by perspective.

ALBERT: But it's my bridge——

FRASER: You think only of yourself—you see yourself as the centre, whereas I know that I am not placed at all——

ALBERT: There are other bridges—bigger——

FRASER (*listening*): What's that?

ALBERT: San Francisco—Sydney——

FRASER: Listen.

ALBERT: Brooklyn—there's a place for you——

FRASER: Listen!

ALBERT: —but I was here first—this is mine——

(*He tails off as there is the faintest sound of 1,800 men marching, whistling 'Colonel Bogey'.*)

FRASER: There's an army on the march. . . .

ALBERT: So they're coming. . . .

FRASER: A solid phalanx moving squarely up the road, an officer at the head. . . .

ALBERT: Fitch.

FRASER: But they're not soldiers.

ALBERT: He's mad.

FRASER (*appalled*): They're just—people.

ALBERT (*shouts—to the people*): Go away!

FRASER: Coming here.

ALBERT: Halt! About turn!

FRASER: They've lined up hundreds and hundreds of ordinary people—the overflow—all the fit men in the prime of life —they're always the ones on the list—preference is given

to the old and the sick, the women and children—when it
comes to the point, it's the young and able-bodied who go
first——

ALBERT: Can't you see—they're taking over!

FRASER: Ten abreast—sixty deep—and another phalanx behind
—and another—successive waves——

(*The whistling is getting louder.*)

—so it has come to this.

ALBERT: They're going to come up!

FRASER: It was the only direction left.

ALBERT: They're going to wheel right——

FITCH (*distant*): Right—wheel!

ALBERT: Off the road and through the gate——

FITCH: Straighten up there!

ALBERT: Up to the end of the bridge, on to the tracks——

FRASER: That's it, then—they have finally run out of space, the
edges have all filled out and now there is only up.

ALBERT: Eighteen-hundred men—flung against me by a madman
Was I so important? Here they come.

(*This is difficult; as the front rank reaches the bridge, the
tramp-tramp of the march should start to ring hollow,
progressively as more and more leave terra firma and reach
the bridge.*)

(*From now, approaching tears.*) I could have done it, given
time——

FRASER: There will be more behind them—the concrete mixers
churn and churn until only a single row of corn grows
between two cities, and is finally ground between their
walls. . . .

ALBERT: They didn't give me a fair chance—I would have
worked nights——

FRASER: They'll all come following—women and children too—
and those that are at the top will be pushed off like
disgraced legionaires——

ALBERT: I had it under control—ahead of schedule——

FRASER: Ah well. But they should be breaking step.

(*Tramp tramp.*)

Like soldiers do when they come to a bridge——